Prayers
around the
Crib

Juliette Levivier

Illustrations by Anne Gravier

MAGNIFICAT® · Ignatius

Table
of Contents

Advent 4

The Advent calendar 6

The Christmas tree 8

The Advent wreath 10

Mistletoe and holly 12

The crib 14

The donkey 16

The ox 18

Mary 20

Joseph 22

Christmas - Jesus is born ! 24

Christmas - Jesus comes to save us 26

Jesus will come again in glory 28

The angels 30

The shepherds 32

The sheep 34

The man who is overwhelmed with joy 36

The miller 38

The other figures 40

The star 42

The three Kings 44

O come, all ye faithful 46

Advent

Prepare the way for the Lord,
make his paths straight.

Luke 3:4

It will be Christmas soon !

In four weeks' time we'll be celebrating the birth of Jesus. These four weeks are called Advent. "Advent" means "arrival". Someone we are waiting for is coming.

We have to get ready for Jesus' coming. We have to decorate the house and buy presents, of course, but above all we have to get our hearts ready.

There's no time to lose ! What do I have to change in my life so that I can welcome Jesus better ?

Lord Jesus,
I want to prepare
myself to receive you
in joy and peace.
Light up the path
that leads me to
Christmas.
Amen.

The Advent calendar

My soul waits for the Lord.

Psalm 130:6

It seems like a very long time till Christmas !

It's really hard to be patient when there are Christmas trees and ads for toys everywhere.

A nice Advent calendar can help you prepare for Christmas: you can open one of the windows every day.

These windows are like the windows of your heart. You open them one by one to let the light of God shine into you. Even if some days your heart stays closed like a shuttered window, the light of the Lord still shines.

Lord, teach me to live peacefully
one day at a time,
not wanting everything right now,
and help me to keep trying.
Help me to stay faithful
to my daily prayer. Amen.

The Christmas tree

Truly, truly, I say to you,
he who believes has eternal life.

John 6:47

There are Christmas trees everywhere: at school, in the streets, in the shops, even in church ! But do you know why we have Christmas trees ? These trees are evergreens. They are a symbol of life because they stay green even in the depths of winter ! We put them in our homes and decorate them to remind ourselves that with Jesus we live forever.

It's great fun to go with Dad or Mom to buy a tree and to take it home and to decorate it ! I want to put the lights on it so that it shines at night. I want to decorate it with ornaments that are round like the earth, because Christmas is for the whole world.

Lord God, I give you thanks
for the life you have given us.
With your help, I want to love
my life and look after it.
I want to live
forever with you.
Amen.

The Advent wreath

You shall be a crown of beauty
in the hand of the Lord.

Isaiah 62:3

At Christmas, Jesus drives the shadows away. He brings us the light. He is the Light.

One beautiful Advent custom is to have a wreath made of evergreen branches and decorated with four big candles. We light one of these candles on each of the four Sundays of Advent. They symbolize the light of Christmas that is coming and the darkness of winter that is disappearing bit by bit.

What can I do so that I can better receive the light of Christmas ? How can I too be a light which lights up the way of the Lord ?

Round like the earth,
green like hope: Lord, how
beautiful your crown is,
shining in the night!
Truly, you are the
King of the universe.
Amen.

Mistletoe and holly

Like a vine I caused loveliness to bud,
and my blossoms became glorious
and abundant fruit.

Sirach 24:17

Isn't holly lovely, with its prickly shiny leaves ? Its red berries liven up winter. A wreath of holly on a front door reminds me of Christ's crown of thorns. All the little red berries between the prickly holly leaves show me that life has triumphed over death.

Mistletoe looks so delicate ! This plant with its nice white berries grows on the branches of trees and feeds on their sap. I feed on the sap of the tree that shelters me, too. That tree is Jesus ! He feeds me with his word and with the Eucharist.

You think of everything, Lord !
The plants that liven up our winter
are so beautiful !
In spite of the cold, in spite of the snow,
they tell us that life is still there,
and that hope is stronger than suffering.
They tell me I can bear fruit
throughout my life.
Amen.

The Crib

*She gave birth to her first-born son and wrapped
him in swaddling cloths,
and laid him in a manger,
because there was no place for them in the inn.*

Luke 2:7

The crib, or manger, is the simple place where Mary laid her baby, Jesus. For a long time, Christians have put scenes in their homes to remind themselves of this. These scenes are made up of little figures of Jesus, Mary, Joseph and a crowd of others.

Each year we carefully wrap up the figures in tissue paper and put them away in their box. It's as if they are sleeping. It makes us very happy when we take them out again – when it's time to wake them up – and place them in a beautiful crib scene ! My heart needs to wake up, too ! I need to be ready when Jesus comes.

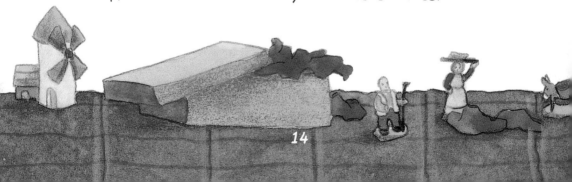

I am ready to welcome you too,
Lord.
My parents,
my brothers and sisters,
my friends,
my neighbors
and I –
we make up a joyful crowd
coming
to adore you.
Keep us all united
to each other.
Amen.

The donkey

Joseph also went up from Galilee,
from the city of Nazareth,
to Judea, to the city of David,
which is called Bethlehem,
because he was of the house and lineage of David.

Luke 2:4

The donkey that carried Mary from Nazareth to Bethlehem was lying on the straw. It was happy to be resting. It had traveled a long way. It was hot and thirsty. It had carried a heavy load but had walked on bravely. Joseph's kind voice and Mary's gentle touch had helped it on its way.

Sometimes people say donkeys are stubborn or stupid. It's true that this donkey didn't understand much, but it was gentle and brave, and was happy to serve.

Sometimes I'm asked to do difficult things too, but I can try my best to help.

Lord, there's a place in your Church
for everyone. Everyone can be a servant.
Everyone has gifts he can bring.
Everyone is important.
Teach me not to look down on anyone
but to recognize each person's worth.
Amen.

The ox

*And this will be a sign for you: you will find
a baby wrapped in swaddling cloth
and lying in a manger.*

Luke 2:12

The ox was lying quietly in its stable when suddenly a tired couple and their donkey arrived. Then a baby started crying. Where had they come from ? Next there was the gentle song of a mother cradling her newborn baby: "Alleluia ! The Lord has done marvels for me."

Then there were even more strangers: angels, shepherds, sheep ! What a lot of people ! How unexpected ! The good beast was happy to welcome them. He was happy to share his humble home.

Now let me also try to welcome people who come and bother me.

Leaning over you, Jesus,
the ox warmed you with his gentle breath.
Like him, by the breath of the Holy Spirit,
I can spread the warmth
of your peace and love
around me.
Amen.

Mary

She gave birth to her first-born son.

Luke 2:7

Mary is the one who says yes to God. She was open to what God asked of her on the day of the Annunciation. Here she is now, ready to welcome Jesus, her tiny baby.

In the crib scene, Mary is usually put in a place of honor beside Jesus. Kneeling before him, in silent wonder, she represents all the mothers of the world.

Do I know how to rest in silent wonder at the presence of Jesus within me ?

Blessed are you, Mary !
You are really blessed among all women !
By your yes to God, Jesus came to live among us.
Teach me to say yes to God each day of my life.
Amen.

Joseph

When Joseph woke from sleep, he did as the angel of the Lord commanded him.

Matthew 1:24

Standing near Mary, Joseph prays and keeps watch. He doesn't speak much. Like all the fathers of the world who are represented by him, he watches over the child. Joseph leans on God and trustingly obeys him.

I don't always like to obey ! Obeying God means letting yourself be loved and responding to that love. It means accepting his plan of love for you. We get close to God by obeying his Word and his Church. Truly, obedience is wonderful !

Lord,

I too want to come to you in silence
and offer you my life.
I want to pray in silence,
without speaking,
just contemplating you,
letting myself be guided,
letting myself be loved,
so that every day of my life
I may do what you ask of me.
Amen.

Christmas –
Jesus is born !

She will give birth to a son and you must name him Jesus, because he is the one who is to save his people from their sins.

Matthew 1:21

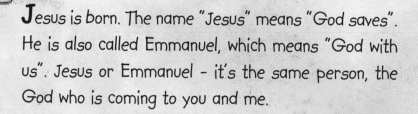

Jesus is born. The name "Jesus" means "God saves". He is also called Emmanuel, which means "God with us". Jesus or Emmanuel – it's the same person, the God who is coming to you and me.

I put Jesus in the crib in the center of the scene. All the other figures are turned toward him.

Let's look at him, adore him, stay close to him. May we be filled with his presence.

A child is born.
He is our God.
He is our Savior.
Alleluia !

Christmas – Jesus comes to save us

Behold your God... He will come and save you.

Isaiah 35:4

Christmas is the great feast that celebrates the birth of Jesus, the Son of God made man. It's like a birthday... with more than 2000 candles ! The present is Jesus himself ! He brings us the love of God. He comes to save us from sin and death. He is the Savior the world has been waiting for, for so long.

I've been waiting a long time too ! Four whole weeks. That's a long time ! Today it's wonderful to celebrate with Jesus and to rejoice with all those I love.

Thank you, Lord God
for giving us
Jesus, your Son.
He is your Word.
He is your love.
He comes to give us his life,
to give us true Life !
Amen.

Jesus will come again in glory

They will see the Son of man coming on the clouds of heaven with power and great glory.

Matthew 24:30

Christmas time comes every year. The Advent wreath reminds me that Jesus will also come again. Advent is not just waiting for Christmas, but also waiting for Jesus to return.

Jesus will come again in glory, not as a poor and weak baby, but with all the majesty and power of a king. His reign will have no end. He will be king for all eternity.

To save me,
you came as a tiny baby;
you died on the cross;
you rose again.
When you come again on the clouds,
you will see how I have tried to love you
in all my words and actions.
Amen.

The angels

For behold, I bring you good news of a great joy
which will come to all the people;
for to you is born this day in the city of David a
Savior, who is Christ the Lord

Luke 2:10-11

How noisy these angels are ! With all their songs and trumpets, they're going to end up waking the baby Jesus. No, he's still sleeping peacefully. The shepherds are astounded by these joyful messengers.

The angels give glory to God. They sing of his marvels and teach us to praise him.

Singing is beautiful ! They say that "singing is praying twice". So I won't hesitate to join my voice with the angels, singing and praising God.

Blessed are you, Lord, for the angels !
They sing of your glory without end.
They sing your praise without end !
I want to sing with them:
"Glory to God in the highest."
Amen.

The shepherds

They went with haste, and found Mary and Joseph,
and the baby lying in a manger.

Luke 2:16

The poor shepherds were terrified. They rubbed their eyes. They couldn't believe their ears.

"Where have all these angels come from ? What's this great joy they're announcing ? A Savior ? Born this evening ? Unbelievable !" Astonished and a bit worried, they hurried off to see Jesus. These poor simple shepherds were the first to visit him.

When they left they were very happy and told everyone they met what they had heard and seen. Great joy like this needs to be shared...

I haven't seen Jesus, but I know he is the Son of God and can witness to his love.

Lord, you see that I am only a child,
but you came down from heaven
for little children
and for the humble and lowly !
You came for me.
You came to save me.
Thank you for giving me
peace and joy this Christmas.
Amen.

The sheep

The Lord is my shepherd,
I shall not want;
he makes me lie down in green pastures

Psalm 23:1-2

The sheep in the crib scene are like people who are pure in heart. They came to Jesus with trust.

The sheep came with all that they had - just their wool for knitting into little socks to keep a baby's feet warm !

I too am like a sheep. Jesus is my shepherd ! He guides me and leads me. He looks for me when I am lost.

Let me bring to the crib all that I am and all that I have. It's nothing extraordinary. But for God I am special because I am his child !

Lord, you are my shepherd !
Protect me from evil and from sin.
Show me the way of joy and peace.
Lead me to happiness,
the happiness of living with you forever.
Amen.

The man who is overwhelmed with joy

Blessed are the pure in heart;
for they shall see God.

In some countries there is another figure in the crib scene. He is overwhelmed by what he has just discovered. He is standing there with his arms wide-open. He is still wearing a night cap because he has just gotten out of bed, and he is running to see Jesus. He has a simple heart, and he is rejoicing at Jesus' birth. He has nothing to give Jesus except his heart, which is full of love. But isn't that the best gift of all ?

Am I ready to welcome Jesus with all my heart ?

I don't have a lot to offer him either. Maybe I have nothing to offer at all. But wait a minute: I can offer him my joy and my smile and my care for others and all the little things I do out of love !

Give me a pure and simple heart,
a joyful heart, open to your love,
overwhelmed by your wonders !
Open my heart to your presence,
open my heart to my brothers and sisters.
I only have my heart to offer you, Lord,
but I give every bit of it to you !
Amen.

The miller

Give us each day our daily bread.

Luke 11:3

Often there is another figure in the crib scene: the miller, dressed in his best clothes and with a cotton hat on his head. He is carrying a large sack of flour on his shoulder to give to Jesus. The flour represents all his work. With his flour, one could make enough bread to feed everyone there.

Bread is a very good thing ! Jesus himself is the Bread of Life. He feeds my soul and gives me Life.

Like the miller, I can offer Jesus my work: my efforts to be good and to do well both at school and at home. I can also offer the ways I help spread the good news of Jesus by being kind to everyone.

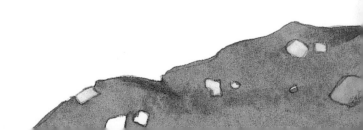

Lord, you invite me to your table.
When I share in the bread of the Eucharist
with my brothers and sisters,
it is you, Lord, who come to me.
You give yourself to me.
You are present in me.
Thank you, Lord.
Amen.

The other figures

A great multitude, hearing all that he did,
came to him.

Mark 3:8

You can put many other figures in the crib scene. They can represent the people of God, all those throughout history who, beginning with Abraham, have been waiting for the Messiah. They also represent all the people who have ever believed that Jesus is their Savior.

What a lot of people ! And yet, Jesus knows each one by name. He loves each one with a special love.

I'm just like a little figure in the crib scene too. Jesus sees me and knows me. He calls me to live with him forever ! My name too is written in heaven !

Lord, so many people
are looking for the truth.
So many people
are looking for you.
Reveal your love
to all the peoples of the earth,
so that they can give you glory together.
Amen.

The star

We have seen his star in the East
and have come to worship him.

Matthew 2:2

The stars are so beautiful, so mysterious and far away. They shine at night to guide travellers and fill the sky with their light.

The star that guided the kings to Jesus shone so brightly that they couldn't stop themselves from following it. They didn't really know where it was leading them, but they put their trust in it !

Jesus is the light that shines for all men and guides them to God. Could I be like a star, showing others the path that leads to Jesus ?

Lord, be my star.
When I am in the dark,
when my heart is darkened
by doubt, sadness and sin,
be the light shining before me !
Amen.

The three Kings

They saw the child with Mary his mother,
and they fell down and worshiped him.

Matthew 2:11

Aren't the kings handsome ! Aren't they majestic with their presents and their jewels ! Aren't their clothes colorful !

They've come from so far away, they've taken so much trouble, they've left everything to see Jesus and to give him praise. They are so great, and he is so small. But there they are, kneeling in front of Jesus; they know that he is the King of kings.

They invite me to set off on a journey too, to leave everything and go to meet Jesus. But where will I find gold, frankincense and myrrh ?

44

Lord Jesus, the kings bow down
before you even though
you are just a little baby.
But you too are a king !
You are the King of the universe.
You are the King of my heart.
I come to kneel down before you.
Amen.

O come all ye faithful

O come, all ye faithful,
Joyful and triumphant,
O come ye, O come ye to Bethlehem.
Come and behold him
Born the King of angels.

O come let us adore Him, (x 3)
Christ the Lord.

God of God,
Light of Light,
Lo ! he abhors not the Virgin's womb:
Very God,
begotten, not created.

See how the shepherds,
Summoned to his cradle,
Leaving their flocks, draw nigh to gaze.
We too will thither
Bend our joyful footsteps.

Lo! star-led chieftains,
Magi, Christ adoring,
Offer him incense, gold, and myrrh.
We to the Christ Child
Bring our hearts' oblations.

Splendor Immortal,
Son of God Eternal,
Now hidden in mortal flesh our eyes shall view.
See there the Infant,
Swaddling clothes enfold him.

Child, for us sinners
Poor and in the manger,
We would embrace thee, with love and awe.
Who would not love thee,
loving us so dearly ?

Sing, choirs of angels;
Sing in exaltation,
Sing, all ye citizens of heaven above:
Glory to God,
In the highest.

Yea, Lord, we greet thee !
Born this happy morning,
Jesus, to thee be glory given;
Word of the Father,
Now in flesh appearing.

Cover illustration by Anne Gravier

Original French edition:
Prier autour de la crèche

© 2006 by Edifa-Mame, Paris
© 2012 by Ignatius Press, San Francisco • Magnificat USA LLC, New York
All rights reserved.
ISBN Ignatius Press 978-1-58617-773-7 • ISBN Magnificat 978-1-936260-47-8
The trademark Magnificat depicted in this publication is used under license
from and is the exclusive property of Magnificat Central Service Team, Inc.,
A Ministry to Catholic Women, and may not be used without its written consent.

Printed by Friesens on August 24, 2012
Job Number MGN 77140
Printed in Canada, in compliance with the Consumer Protection Safety Act of 2008.